Heart's Ledger

Navigating the Emotional Currency of Economics

By

Travis Jon Riley

Heart's Ledger Navigating the Emotional Currency of Economics

Travis Jon Riley

Published by TRAVIS JON RILEY, 2023.

Table of Contents

Emotional Economics
The Heart's Role in Your Wallet

An excitement rushes through you when you pass a store and see an article of apparel or a device you've been eyeing. Your heartbeat picks up speed. Yet why? Is it just the thought of getting something brand-new? Or does it go deeper than that, connected to a reservoir of feelings, painful memories, and ingrained social norms? Money isn't merely a means to an end for many people. It is profoundly entwined with our minds in ways that the majority of us hardly understand. It serves as an emotional tool, and occasionally even an emotional crutch. You have arrived in the world of emotional economics.

A common misconception about the world of finance is that it is a complex, cold place made of statistics, facts, and emotionless computations. We've been trained to think that the best financial choices are ones that are rational, objective, and analytical. But if you look a little closer, behind the immaculate spreadsheets and calculators, you'll discover a human heart that beats with emotions, memories, hopes, and fears. This is the start of our tale.

As old as money itself, the relationship between money and emotion is a long one. Consider the times when a man may provide the family of a prospective bride with a dowry. That dowry wasn't simply money; it was also a symbol of love, a guarantee of safety, and occasionally a source of pride or conflict. Even while our financial transactions of today may look different, their emotional foundations are pretty similar.

Why does one person spend lavishly while the other saves every penny? Why might one person view stock market declines as a purchasing opportunity while another views the same event as a catastrophic loss and sells all of their investments in a fit of panic? Less in the field of economics and more in the field of psychology are the solutions.

Psychologists have historically divided human emotions into fundamental groups. Each emotion has the potential to affect, if not control, our financial decisions. The excitement of finding a $20 bill on the sidewalk, the grief following a monetary loss, the worry of an upcoming expensive medical procedure, or the jealousy of viewing a friend's extravagant vacation images on social media.

Despite being universal, these feelings are also very personal. Whether you are aware of it or not, a variety of circumstances, including childhood memories, past financial triumphs and traumas, cultural pressures, personal aspirations, and frequently a desire for approval or a sense of belonging, have shaped your relationship with money. In many respects, money has evolved into a mirror that shows not only the state of our finances but also our emotional, psychological, and even spiritual well-being.

Understanding this complex dance between money and emotion, however, is not about assigning blame or making snap decisions. It has to do with getting clear. It involves using the compass of reason and the anchor of emotional awareness to steer across the huge ocean of financial decisions. We shall set out on a journey to investigate these intricate connections, the unseen forces that pull on our emotions even as we open our wallets, in the pages that follow.

This investigation will be revelatory for some readers, illuminating patterns and behaviors that had previously been obscured. Others might see it as confirmation of what they already knew but were unable to express. Others, however, may find it to be a road map to a more amicable relationship with their money, bridging the chasm between the heart and the bank account.

The goal of "Emotional Economics" is not to take emotions out of our financial calculations because that would be impractical and, in some cases, undesirable. Our lives take on more color thanks to our emotions, which also enrich our experiences and frequently lead us to our most genuine selves. Instead, the objective is to comprehend, control, and occasionally restrain these emotions so that they aid rather than hinder us.

You could come across tales and situations as you read the pages that make you nod in recognition or sigh in understanding. You might also come across stories that take place in the distant past, but they too have lessons to teach you about the complex web of human emotion and how it affects our financial lives.

We are here to investigate the grays—the messy, nuanced, and beautiful interaction of the heart's wishes and the wallet's realities—in a world that increasingly demands black-and-white solutions. So let's start this journey into the human heart and spirit, where real choices are made and real lives are shaped, rather than merely the realm of money. You've arrived at "Emotional Economics."

Chapter 1:
Setting the Stage

Two things have been consistent throughout human history: emotion and trade. From the early barter systems to the sophisticated financial networks of today, the act of exchanging commodities and services has been motivated by a variety of emotions in addition to needs. Every financial transaction, no matter how great or small, contains a shadow of these emotions: happiness, anxiety, hope, desperation, and ambition.

A Glimpse into the Past

In addition to being places of trade, ancient markets, with their stalls stocked with fabrics, spices, and antiquities, were also thriving theatre's of human emotion. These feelings have been acted out for millennia: the happiness in a child's eyes when her father buys her a tasty treat; the tense discussions between a merchant and a skeptic; and the anxiety of a farmer hoping his crops sell before sunset.

Think of Rome in antiquity, a society renowned for its sophisticated marketplaces and financial structures. Roman society was class-based, and social position was frequently determined by one's financial situation. The affluent elites flaunted their wealth with expensive feasts, opulent homes, and pricey attire. Was this only for solace? Not completely. It was about displaying pride, making a power play, and looking for approval—deeply emotional goals. The regular people, meanwhile, scrimped and saved because they were afraid of unforeseen disasters and hopeful for a brighter tomorrow.

Economics vs. Emotional Economics

As a discipline, traditional economics assumes that people are logical entities. The underlying premise of classical economic theories is that individuals constantly act to maximize gains and minimize losses. But real-life situations repeatedly refute this idea.

Consider the famed Tulip Mania in the Netherlands during the 17th century. Tulip bulbs briefly rose to popularity, with prices rocketing to astonishing heights. Some bulbs reportedly sold for the price of a fancy home at the height of this bubble. Was this sensible? Without a doubt not, strictly speaking. The intrinsic value of the tulip bulbs did not support these excessive costs. However, the phenomenon begins to make more sense when we take into account human emotions, such as the desire to join in the most recent trend, the pleasure of speculating, and the fear of losing out. It wasn't simply the appeal of the tulip that drew people in; it was also the game's intoxicating draw, the elation of possible wealth, and the fear of being left out.

These behavioral oddities are beginning to be taken into account in modern economic theory. The field of behavioral economics, which combines psychological knowledge with economic theory, accepts that people frequently behave irrationally. Our financial decisions can be significantly influenced by emotions, prejudices, and cultural influences.

The Emotional Spectrum

It's critical to understand that our relationship with money is not exclusively based on simple input-output equations or objective, cold facts. Our financial choices frequently reflect a range of emotions:

Happy and content: Consider the last time you bought something that made you happy. Was it a pricey device? a jewelry item? A book? Frequently, the joy experienced after making such purchases extends beyond the material object. It fulfills a deeper emotional need by serving as a reward for effort, a vehicle for self-expression, or possibly a link to a treasured memory.

Anxiety & Fear: On the other hand, fear can be a strong motivator for making financial decisions. Aversion to investments, excessive saving, and even hoarding are all symptoms of fears such as those of poverty, being left behind, and unforeseen bills.

Desire and Hope: Our financial decisions may be influenced by our hopes for a better future and the accomplishment of specific life goals. Financial choices involving education investments, property purchases, and business ventures are all motivated by optimism.

An elongated sword

Emotions are just what they are; they are neither nice nor harmful. They may serve as strong inspirations that drive us to achieve excellence. But if left uncontrolled, they can also spell disaster. The first step in learning emotional economics is to recognize and comprehend the emotional underpinnings of our financial decisions.

For instance, a businessperson might finance a project that is motivated by enthusiasm and sincere confidence in the goods. This psychological link may encourage persistence and result in achievement. But what if the entrepreneur's emotions impair judgment and keep him or her from recognizing obvious market signs that the business is doomed to fail? In this situation, feelings can result in financial ruin.

A Balancing Act

Remember this as we dig further into the domain of emotional economics: ignorance, not emotions, is the enemy of wise financial judgment. We can strike a balance by comprehending, identifying, and occasionally confronting our emotional reactions to make financial decisions that speak to our hearts and make sense to our minds.

In the chapters that follow, we'll go into great detail about each emotion, looking at where it came from, how it shows up in our financial life, and how to use it to our advantage. This journey may affect more than just how you view money; it may also alter how you view yourself.

Chapter 2
The Spectrum of Emotions

The diversity and colors of our emotions are what define us as humans. They influence how we communicate, how we remember things, and how we make decisions—whether they be financial, professional, or personal. Understanding the range of our emotional experiences is crucial before one can properly comprehend emotional economics. The huge range of human emotions will be examined in this chapter, together with their causes, expressions, and unmistakable effects on our financial psyche.

The Foundations of Emotion

It's important to realize that emotions are more than just ephemeral feelings before we delve further. They are intricate psychological states that are frequently based on our evolutionary past and created to aid us in navigating a constantly shifting environment. At some point along our evolutionary path, each emotion—the rush of delight, the sting of melancholy, the chills of fear—has contributed to our survival and spread.

Joy and Pleasure

From an evolutionary perspective, happiness served as a reward system. The brain generated chemicals that made people feel good when our ancestors did things that helped them survive, like finding food or making partnerships.

Happiness is frequently associated with benefits in the world of money. Consider perks, unanticipated riches, or profitable investments. The prospect of happiness can be a potent incentive that drives people to pursue financial achievement. However, it can also result in impulsive behavior, such as overspending on unnecessary products just for the excitement of it.

Sadness and Loss

Although it may seem paradoxical, social connectedness is the source of sadness. When someone was depressed, other group members would frequently show sympathy and support, guaranteeing that the person would be taken care of and shielded from harm.

Sadness is frequently brought on by financial setbacks, missed chances, or growing indebtedness. Some people may find this feeling to be paralyzing, making them cautious of potential financial dangers. It can, however, also serve as a potent lesson that instills care and prudence.

Fear and Anxiety

Our desire to protect ourselves makes fear one of the most basic human emotions. Fear arose, causing immediate reaction actions in response to an oncoming predator, a competing tribe, or natural disasters.

Fear can be sparked by the erratic nature of the financial markets, the unpredictability of investments, or the prospect of losing one's employment. This feeling may act as a defense mechanism, encouraging us to diversify our investments or save for a rainy day. However, overwhelming fear can also result in lost chances and stagnation.

Anger and Frustration

Perceived threats to status or territory were the most common causes of anger. It ensured survival and supremacy by preparing the body for conflict.

Anger can be expressed financially if one feels cheated, is underpaid in a transaction, or is subject to unfair financial circumstances. Uncontrolled anger can result in rash, unwise judgments even if it can occasionally lead to activism, demanding just compensation or better financial regulations.

Surprise and Speculation

The sense of surprise served as a rapid reset button. Rapid reevaluation and action were needed in response to unexpected events to ensure survival in the face of unknown threats or possibilities.

In financial situations, surprise frequently manifests as swift market shifts, unanticipated windfalls, or unplanned bills. The emotional basis may fuel rapid adaptation and may involve using a sudden market boom as an example. But it can also result in speculative actions, where the allure of the unknowable motivates dangerous bets.

Envy and Desire

Envy encouraged individuals to seek out the resources, partners, or abilities that others possessed, ensuring competition and advancing evolution.

In a society where social media is emphasized, envy frequently manifests as a longing for the things, adventures, or lifestyles that peers are showcasing. Envy can inspire people to work toward improving their financial circumstances, but unrestrained envy can also result in careless spending or living beyond one's means.

Understanding the Interplay

Even though we've examined each emotion separately, it's important to understand that they rarely function independently. The excitement of a promotion might coexist with the worry of taking on more responsibility. Anger directed at individuals seen as accountable may add to the misery of a financial loss. Our financial decisions are frequently influenced by this intricate interplay, this emotional concoction.

Further influencing these feelings are our specific histories, upbringings, cultural backgrounds, and experiences. Depending on their emotional backgrounds and worldviews, two people may react differently to the same financial situation.

Embracing the Spectrum

The first step to learning emotional economics is to understand the range of emotions. Making wise choices requires being aware of the causes, symptoms, and behaviors that follow. Instead of stifling feelings, one should learn to harness them positively.

As we continue on our journey, we'll delve deeper into each person's emotions and explore ways to harness their strength so that we may make financial decisions that are not just rational but also emotionally intelligent. Every financial decision ultimately reflects who we are, what we have gone through, and where we hope to go.

Chapter 3
The Dual Power of Fear and Hope

Many of our actions, especially those involving money, are governed by a delicate balance between fear and hope. Although they initially seem to be in opposition to one another, the complex dance between these two emotions provides a distinct environment for our financial behaviors. In this chapter, we'll delve deeply into both, not as competing but rather as complimentary elements that influence how we view money.

Fear: The Protective Shadow

Fear is fundamentally a defense mechanism. It's a primal emotion that dates back to the beginning of time and was created to protect us from danger. Fear protects us from potential danger, whether we are managing the complexity of a turbulent stock market today or facing a prowling predator in ancient times.

Fear frequently takes the form of prudence in financial circumstances. It might dissuade someone from making a dangerous venture, motivate someone else to preserve money for unforeseen difficulties, or cause someone to second-guess making a large buy.

Risk Aversion: A common financial behavior stemming from fear is the aversion to risk. Fear-driven people favor secure, reliable, and predictable financial products, even if it results in possibly lower returns.

Over-caution: Although a certain amount of caution is advantageous, exercising excessive caution might result in the loss of chances. For instance, someone might refrain from making any investments out of fear of suffering a loss or missing out on prospective rewards.

Debt Phobia: Fear can also make people excessively apprehensive of taking on any kind of debt, even when doing so could be advantageous for investments or big-ticket purchases like homes or schools.

Hope: The Beacon of Possibilities

The emotion that propels us ahead is hope. It is the hope for a brighter future, the confidence in the opportunities that lay ahead, and the drive behind development and expansion.

Hope encourages people to take risks in the world of money. It is what motivates people to invest in startups, choose to go to college even though it is expensive, or decide to buy a house with the hope of having a happy future.

Risk-Taking: Hope can motivate people to take calculated risks by encouraging them to invest in lucrative businesses or markets in the hopes of seeing a profit.

Hope is also the cornerstone of future investments, whether they involve putting money down for retirement, getting insurance, or investing in one's abilities and education.

Over-optimism: Just as fear can lead to over-caution, excessive hope can sometimes blur reality, leading individuals to make overly optimistic financial decisions without adequately gauging risks.

The Interplay: Balancing Hope and Fear

Most people's financial journeys are influenced by a dance between hope and anxiety rather than just one emotion.

Making Balanced Decisions: Fear and hope should ideally serve as counterbalances. While fear should instill a sense of caution, ensuring that actions are well-calibrated and dangers are understood, hope should encourage one to pursue opportunities.

Economic Cycles and Emotions: It's interesting to note that the relative strength of hope and fear is frequently influenced by the overall economic climate. Collective optimism frequently triumphs over collective anxiety in flourishing economies, encouraging expanding actions like increasing investment and spending. In contrast, during recessions, fear takes center stage and steers people and institutions in the direction of cautious financial decisions.

Personal Financial Trajectories: A person's prior experiences have a big impact on how much hope there is compared to how much fear there is. Someone who has experienced significant financial losses can be too afraid, whereas someone who has continuously experienced financial success might be more motivated by hope.

Harnessing Fear and Hope

It's essential to use fear and hope's power for overall financial welfare; understanding them is more than just a theoretical exercise.

Self-awareness: Start by becoming conscious of your prejudices. Do you tend to make more financial decisions out of fear or hope? Recognizing this might help you see possibilities and hazards through a better perspective.

Education in Finance: Arm yourself with knowledge. While emotions may be a factor in decisions, having a good basis in financial markets, instruments, and economic trends can help to ensure that these influences are not the only factors at play.

Different Approaches: Develop a variety of financial methods to strike a balance between hope and worry. While some of your financial resources can be retained in safe, low-risk investments, other parts of your assets can be put towards higher-risk, higher-reward ventures.

Embracing the Dual Dance

Although they may seem incongruous, hope and fear represent the yin and yang of our financial emotions. A lack of one might result in either reckless abandonment or debilitating immobility. Together, they can direct us toward choices that are both morally right and economically wise.

It's essential to keep in mind that all emotions, including fear and hope, have their proper context as we move forward with our exploration of emotional economics. They are our navigators, leading us through the complex web of choices that determine our financial destinies. They aren't just fellow travelers on our financial voyage.

Chapter 4
The Foundations of Financial Interactions

Skepticism and Trust

Two emotions stand out in the complex ballet of financial decisions: trust and suspicion. These are not merely ephemeral feelings; rather, they are fundamental emotions that form the basis of human interactions, particularly in a world where faceless transactions and electronic exchanges predominate. Let's explore these emotions' functions and how they affect our financial futures.

Trust: The Foundation of Commerce

Human civilization is made of a fabric that includes trust. Our forebears organized tribes, exchanged goods, and established trustworthy communities. It is the conviction that another person or thing will behave in a dependable, predictable, and mutually advantageous way.

Whether it's making an internet purchase, investing in mutual funds, or making a bank deposit, trust is the basis of every financial transaction.

Brand Loyalty: Brand loyalty is frequently fueled by trust. When a business continuously provides quality, it builds consumer trust and receives their business again and again.

Financial Institutions: Where people deposit their hard-earned money or where they decide to invest depends on their trust in financial institutions, such as banks or investment businesses.

Brokers and Advisers: A reputable broker or financial advisor may have lifelong clients. For relationships to last, both parties must feel that the other is looking out for their best interests.

Skepticism: The Shield of Protection

Skepticism ensures safety while trust fosters the development of relationships. It is the emotion that encourages skepticism, caution, and the examination of intentions. Skepticism evolved to defend our ancestors from potential dangers or deception.

Skepticism serves as a defense in financial situations against fraud, agreements that seem too good to be true, and dubious investments.

Avoiding Scams: People can avoid falling for financial scams or other fraudulent schemes by exercising a healthy degree of skepticism.

Analyzing Investments: Skepticism encourages people to analyze the risks, rewards, and legitimacy of an opportunity before investing.

Negotiations: Whether buying a car, a house or negotiating a salary, skepticism can ensure that individuals don't just take things at face value but engage in deeper deliberation.

Skepticism vs. Faith

Finding the ideal mix between trust and skepticism is crucial for having a stable financial future.

Erosion of Trust: Trust, once lost, is challenging to regain. Financial organizations that violate the confidence of their customers, whether through obfuscated fees, poor management, or unethical behavior, frequently suffer long-term consequences.

Skepticism that paralyzes: Skepticism, while protective, can paralyze when it becomes excessive. Due to an ingrained doubt in their sincerity, people may pass up on real opportunities.

Building Trust: Trust isn't just given; it's developed. Trust is developed through time, whether it be through financial institutions being open and honest in their dealings or brands constantly keeping their promises.

Educated Skepticism: Skepticism shouldn't merely be unfounded doubt; it should be informed by knowledge. Education and financial literacy may make sure that skepticism is used wisely, questioning where it is necessary and accepting when confirmation is obvious.

Applications to the Real World

Cryptocurrencies: The struggle between trust and skepticism is clear in the world of digital currency. While many people have faith in the technology and decentralized nature of cryptocurrencies, others are still wary of their volatility and lack of regulation.

Online retail: E-commerce platforms have devoted years to establishing confidence by guaranteeing safe transactions, simple returns, and quality control. However, new competitors entering the market or instances of fraud raise doubt.

Crowdfunding: Websites like Kickstarter or GoFundMe rely heavily on user trust to function. Financial support for an idea or cause is given by backers who believe in it. However, unsuccessful or wasteful enterprises might increase distrust of such platforms.

Finding Your Way Through the Twin Pillars

The two sides of a river, trust, and skepticism, govern the course of our financial relationships. Skepticism assures safety, prudence, and due diligence whereas trust promotes development, connection, and prosperity.

The balance between trust and skepticism will be crucial as we become more integrated into a global financial ecosystem, where interactions cross continents and technology dissolves old boundaries. It is about informed faith and educated inquiry, not about mindlessly believing or cynically doubting.

In the upcoming chapters, we'll examine tools, strategies, and ways of thinking that can help strike the correct balance, making sure that while our financial path is founded on emotion, it is also grounded in knowledge and understanding.

Chapter 5
The Temporal Battle Between Today's Pleasure and Tomorrow's Security

Numerous dichotomies that influence how we make financial decisions have been addressed during our exploration of emotional economics. The conflict that exists within us between the draw of instant enjoyment and the pull of securing a more secure future may be one of the most fascinating of these conflicts. To discover a balanced course of action, this chapter digs into this internal struggle, explaining its causes, ramifications, and solutions.

The Lure of Instant Gratification

Our biology is predisposed to wanting instant fulfillment. In terms of evolution, our ancestors were more focused on immediate survival than on long-term planning. The dopamine rush that comes from immediately gratifying a need or desire is strong and alluring.

Financial Manifestation: In today's world, this manifests as overspending on luxury goods, making hasty purchases, or prioritizing momentary pleasures above long-term profits.

Consumer Culture: This innate tendency is amplified by our contemporary consumer culture, which places a strong focus on the "new," "now," and "novel." The temptation to overindulge now and regret it later is constant due to easy access to credit and the appeal of advertising.

Current Financial Products: Products that directly pander to this urge for rapid pleasure include credit cards and buy-now-pay-later plans. They make it possible to buy anything right away with the expectation that you will pay for it later.

Emotional Highs: The satisfaction of a recent purchase, the excitement of a trip, or the pleasure of a fine meal all produce instant emotional highs that reinforce the preference for the present over the future.

The Hope for Security in the Future

Nevertheless, as human lifespans lengthened and civilizations became more complicated, a parallel pull emerged—the requirement to plan, safeguard, and protect one's future. This is the world of foresight, of postponing present desires in favor of future necessities.

Financial Manifestation: This attitude motivates retirement savings, asset investments, insurance purchases, and even forgoing luxuries to fund children's education.

The Retirement Dream: For many, saving money, making smart investments, and diligent planning are compelling incentives to retire comfortably and worry-free.

Experiences Over Assets: While activities bring happiness right away, assets like gold, stocks, or real estate offer long-term growth and security, making them desirable alternatives for those who are looking ahead.

Security Mesh: Many people create safety nets in the form of health insurance, emergency cash, or diverse investment portfolios since life is unpredictable.

Navigating Today and Tomorrow: It is difficult but necessary to achieve a healthy balance between these conflicting pulls for overall financial wellness.

Budgeting for Balance: A successful budget involves allocating money for today's joys and tomorrow's security. One might feign balance by allocating particular sums for entertainment, travel, or luxury and making sure to make regular payments to savings or investments.

How to Calculate the Time Value of Money: Understanding how compound interest works and how a dollar saved or invested now might be worth much more later on might alter perceptions. It can increase the attraction and tangibility of the promise of future security.

Emotional Resilience: Enhancing emotional resilience helps lessen the irrational desire for instant fulfillment. One can lessen the appeal of rapid rewards by finding satisfaction in simpler things, cultivating gratitude, or seeking emotional highs apart from worldly possessions.

Techniques for Closing the Temporal Gap

The 24-hour Rule: For significant non-essential purchases, implement a 24-hour waiting period. Distinguishing between temporary wants and true necessities during this cooling-off period can frequently bring insight.

Automated Savings: Automation can be a powerful ally. One can make sure that future security is prioritized before current temptations can take hold by setting up automated payments to savings accounts, retirement funds, or investments.

Think about the future: Regularly picturing future objectives, such as a dream house, a world tour after retirement, or a child's graduation, might make them more real and increase motivation to pursue them.

Consult a financial counselor: A financial advisor or counselor can offer an unbiased viewpoint and assist in outlining a course that strikes a balance between short-term desires and long-term objectives.

Accepting the Temporal Dance

The tension between today and tomorrow is a representation of human experience as well as a financial difficulty. We alternate between being present in the now and making plans for the future, between making the most of the present and getting ready for the future.

Recognizing this emotional dance is the first step in the world of finance. We may enjoy both the pleasures of the present and the prospects of the future by comprehending our biases, being aware of outside influences, and arming ourselves with the necessary tools and methods.

We'll keep peeling back the layers of our relationship with money as we explore deeper into emotional economics, revealing the unseen forces that form our financial narratives and providing guidance on how to write one that is in line with our loftiest aspirations and deepest wishes.

Chapter 6
Fear and Hope
The Yin and Yang of Financial Decisions

Every financial journey is laced with both hopeful and fearful times. These two emotions have a significant impact on how we make financial decisions, from the fear of making a risky investment to the excitement of starting a new business. Let's navigate the complex maze of fear and hope, looking at their causes, how they interact, and the significant influence they have on our financial lives.

The Haunting Shadows

Fear is a primitive feeling that has its roots in our ancestors' instinct to recognize and react to danger. It is the body's defensive mechanism, alerting us to prospective threats and urging us to take appropriate action.

This protective emotion can sometimes eclipse our financial environment, causing paralysis, risk aversion, or rash decisions, even though it is useful in many settings.

Market turbulence: Even the smallest indication of a financial crisis or a decline in the value of the stock market can cause panic selling or investor exodus among investors.

labor Security: In a labor market that is always changing, people's fear of losing their jobs might influence their career decisions, steer them into "safe" jobs, or stymie their entrepreneurial aspirations.

FOMO: "Fear of Missing Out" Although it was once thought of as a type of anxiety brought on by social exclusion, FOMO has now permeated financial decisions. Fear of missing a rich investing opportunity or falling behind peers might cause people to make hasty, ignorant judgments.

The Lighthouse of Hope

On the other side, hope is the feeling of expectation, the conviction that the future or the conclusion will be beneficial. It is the force that drives us ahead and fosters ambition, growth, and exploration.

Hope can act as the propellant that propels our financial pursuits forward, encouraging investments, advancing our financial objectives, and inspiring us to overcome obstacles.

Investing in the Future: The act of investing, be it in stocks, real estate, or startups, is rooted in hope. It is the conviction that money invested now will increase and produce profits down the road.

Career Aspirations: In the hope of greater financial prospects, people pursue further education, look for promotions, or even shift careers.

Economic Hope: Hope can influence consumer confidence on a bigger scale. People are more likely to spend, invest, and promote economic growth when they have faith in the future of the economy.

Hope Inspires, Fear Checks

Though seemingly at odds, fear, and hope often operate in tandem, each influencing and moderating the other.

Risk assessment: While fear makes sure people do their homework, understand the market, and have a backup plan, hope may spur people to launch a business.

Financial Planning: Hope propels people to set ambitious financial goals, like buying a dream home or retiring early. In contrast, fear compels people to take precautions, such as making sure they have insurance, emergency savings, and a variety of assets.

Market Behavior: Bull runs in stock markets can be fueled by hope, pushing up stock prices, while corrections can be sparked by fear, keeping prices within reasonable bounds.

Obtaining Balance: Using Hope and Fear

Educate and Empower: Information allays unwarranted worries and provides hope with a strong basis. One can better handle the tension between fear and hope by educating oneself on financial markets, economic principles, and personal finance.

Emotional Intelligence: It is essential to recognize when decisions are influenced by unrestrained fear or naive hope. Financial self-reflection can help spot emotional biases and ensure better rational decision-making.

Diversify and hedge: A balanced financial portfolio is not merely a combination of assets, but also a combination of risk-taking endeavors and anxiety-relieving measures. Bonds or insurance can be seen as safeguards against risks, whereas investments in startups or growth-oriented industries symbolize optimism.

Seek Mentorship: Engaging with financial mentors or advisors can provide an objective perspective. They can give meaning to dreams, allay irrational concerns, and offer advice on how to effectively strike a balance between the two.

Accepting the Emotional Spectrum in Conclusion

Like the traditional yin and yang, fear and hope stand in for the opposing forces that shape our financial journey. While fear makes us cautious, hope makes us move forward. Financial success can be accompanied by emotional fulfillment if these emotions are recognized, respected, and balanced.

We'll go further into more complex emotions, the cultural structures that magnify them, and the methods to harness their power as we continue our investigation into emotional economics. Because of the emotional nature of our relationship with money, which shapes not only our bank accounts but also our life narratives, it is not just a transactional relationship.

Chapter 7
Trust and Money
Building Financial Bridges

The trust serves as a golden thread in the rich tapestry of our financial life, tying the various strands of our economic transactions together. This feeling has a significant and frequently unacknowledged influence on our financial decisions, whether it is faith in financial institutions, investment possibilities, or our judgment. Let's set out on a trip to comprehend the meanings of trust, the basis upon which it rests, and the connections it creates in our financial world.

The Facets of Trust

Trust is a feeling that has evolved through thousands of years as people have discovered the advantages of working together. Trust serves as the glue that holds people together in a complex society, enabling group projects and reciprocal development.

In the world of money, trust takes many different forms and influences behavior, decisions, and the basic framework of economic systems.

Institutional trust: This is our belief in financial regulators, insurance providers, and banks. It supports our propensity to make deposits, obtain loans, or make market investments.

Personal Trust: This is confidence in oneself, our financial knowledge, our sense of judgment, and the decisions we make. It serves as the basis for self-directed investments, company ventures, or significant financial decisions.

Personal Trust: Every financial transaction is, at its foundation, a human relationship. Interpersonal trust is our belief in business partners, financial advisors, or even in the people we buy or sell to.

When Trust Deteriorates

Economic Recessions: A serious financial crisis, such as the one in 2008, frequently arises from (and contributes to) a loss of trust. When confidence in institutions declines, it may result in bank robberies, less investment, and a general downturn in the economy.

Personal Financial Setbacks: Misjudgments, like a bad investment or a business failure, can shatter personal trust. It may discourage people from making more investments or starting their businesses.

Frauds and scams: Ponzi schemes and other false investment possibilities are examples of financial frauds that not only cause cash losses but also severely damage interpersonal trust, leaving victims leery of new financial dealings.

Reestablishing and Creating Trust

Transparency: Establishing trust requires both individuals and institutions to be upfront about their financial intentions and to disclose their financial health. Trust can be developed, for example, by a bank being open about its assets and liabilities or an investment opportunity providing clear details.

Education and Empowerment: Knowledge is frequently the first step in developing personal trust. Programs, courses, or simply individual research on financial matters can increase confidence in one's financial judgment.

Regulation and Oversight: Strict financial oversight procedures, oversight systems, and fraud-punishment laws help strengthen institutional confidence. People can trust the system because they know there is a watchdog.

Reputation: In the financial industry, reputation is a priceless asset. Those organizations or people who have a track record of morality, dependability, and ethical conduct are inherently more trustworthy.

Personal Experience: Successful financial outcomes strengthen interpersonal and personal trust, whether they result from sensible financial decisions or successful

Company Decisions: Trust levels can be strongly influenced by success stories, recommendations from others, and even personal endorsements.

The Financial Benefits of Trust

Fluid Markets: Strong levels of trust provide smooth operation of the financial markets. As a result of increased investor engagement and preserved liquidity, the economy is kept stable.

Growth and Innovation: Trust encourages an enterprising spirit. Individuals are more inclined to innovate, take prudent risks, and promote economic progress when they trust their gut feelings and the financial system.

Social Cohesion: Beyond just economic benefits, trust leads to societal cohesion. Reliable financial systems promote social cohesion, assure fair growth, and lessen economic inequalities.

Trust as the Financial Compass

The intangible emotion of trust works invisibly in the background, controlling the flow of money, influencing decisions, and determining economic outcomes, even if numbers, data, and analytical tools are frequently at the forefront of financial debates.

As we learn more about emotional economics, it becomes clear that our financial narratives are a complicated synthesis of reason and feeling, information and intuition, and research and faith. Accepting this duality, recognizing the importance of feelings like trust, and actively fostering it can open the door to both individual and group economic growth.

Together we will examine more of these emotions, each of which tells its own financial story and weaves a distinctive pattern in the larger financial mosaic.

Chapter 8

Ambition and Contentment

The Two Sides of Financial Fulfillment

Two emotions stand out in the ever-changing dance of our financial lives: ambition and contentment. These two feelings are frequently at odds with one another but are symbiotically linked. The first urges us to move forward and achieve greater heights, while the second calls for us to be at peace with where we are right now. Achieving a complete level of financial well-being requires balancing these emotions. This chapter explores how ambition and satisfaction interact, their ramifications, and the balance we should pursue.

The Ambition Flame

Our innate desire to achieve, stand out from the crowd, and obtain the best resources for survival and reproduction is the source of ambition, a powerful force.

In the modern world, this instinctive drive is focused on accumulating riches, establishing financial independence, and reaching significant economic milestones.

Career Ladder: Professionals climbing the corporate ladder in search of greater jobs, benefits, and salaries are propelled by ambition.

Entrepreneurial Ventures: It's the driving force behind innovators, risk-takers, and visionaries who transform ideas into profitable enterprises.

Gains on Investments: Ambition fuels the urge to diversify into profitable industries, find the next big stock, and watch one's portfolio increase.

The Arms of Satisfaction

A condition of quiet satisfaction known as contentment dates back to a time when humans would revel in the delight of plenty following a successful hunt or harvest, appreciating the little break from the never-ending search for food.

In the modern world, being content means appreciating what we already have and putting up a fight against the constant need to get more.

Living Within Means: This is demonstrated in the lives of people who put their needs before their wants and avoid falling into the consumerist trap.

Value Over Volume: Financially contented People are those who enjoy significant events or purchases rather than accumulating things.

Gratitude and Generosity: People who are content frequently demonstrate gratitude for their financial situation, no matter how little, and have a predisposition for generosity and sharing.

The Problem of Duality

Despite the virtues of both emotions, an imbalance can cause both financial and psychological problems:

Unchecked Ambition: If ambition is overemphasized, it may result in fatigue, unethical decisions, or financial risks that put one's security in danger.

Excessive Contentment: On the flip side, too much contentment might result in complacency, missed opportunities, or stagnation.

Maintaining Balance

Self-awareness: Regular reflection can assist people in determining whether their priorities are too strongly skewed toward ambition or contentment. To achieve balance, one must first have a clear understanding of their beliefs, objectives, and priorities.

Setting Specific Objectives: Contentment defines the pace of the journey while ambition determines the direction. Maintaining balance can be made easier by setting definite, doable, and adaptable financial goals.

Milestones to be honored: Every success, whether it be paying off debt, saving money, or getting a raise, deserves to be recognized. This action encourages satisfaction while recognizing aspiration.

Continuous Learning: The financial world is dynamic. Constant learning keeps satisfaction from turning into ignorance and guarantees that ambition is motivated by knowledge.

Seeking Advice: Peer groups, mentors, and financial advisors can all provide insight to help people strike the right balance between ambition and contentment.

The Wider Consequences

Ambition and satisfaction interact in ways that go beyond money. Our relationships, mental health, and level of life happiness are all influenced by:

Relationship dynamics: While ambition may motivate people to put in more effort at work, thereby securing better futures for their families, it can also strain relationships owing to a lack of time and attention. On the other side, contentment may prioritize family time yet may result in financial limitations.

Mental Health: Overly ambitious people may experience stress, worry, or feelings of inadequacy. Overindulgence could result in a loss of drive or direction.

The Financial Dance of Dual Emotions

Understanding and harmonizing the forces of ambition and satisfaction become crucial as we sail the rough waters of the emotional economy. These opposing feelings, which stand for our want for more and appreciation of the present, influence not just our financial statements but also our life tales.

Our financial journey is a rhythmic dance between striving and enjoying ourselves rather than a straight line. Recognizing this and giving each feeling its proper place can result in a financially prosperous and profoundly rewarding life.

Chapter 9:
Fear and Hope
Navigating the Volatile Waters of Finance

Every financial decision, big or small, is often suspended between two powerful emotions: fear and hope. These emotions, polar yet interdependent, pull us in opposite directions, making our financial journey as unpredictable as it is thrilling. Chapter 9 seeks to explore these two titans of Emotional Economics, decoding their origins, manifestations, and strategies to harness them for better financial outcomes.

The Shadows of Fear

From an evolutionary perspective, fear is primal. It's the ancient alarm system alerting us to threats. While early humans feared predators, we now fear financial ruin, market crashes, or missed opportunities.

Fear in finance is multi-dimensional:

Loss Aversion: Studies show that the pain of losing money is often more intense than the joy of gaining. This fear can make investors overly cautious, missing out on potential gains.

Economic Uncertainty: The trepidation surrounding economic downturns, job losses, or inflation is rooted in fear.

Debt Phobia: Many avoid loans or credit, fearing the cycle of debt, even when leveraging could be beneficial.

The Beacon of Hope

Hope is as ancient as fear. It's the emotional mechanism that kept our ancestors moving forward, searching for better hunting grounds or more fertile lands.

In the context of finance, hope wears several hats:

Investment Optimism: Every stock purchase or property investment carries the hope of appreciation, dividends, or rental income.

Career Aspirations: The belief in a better job, a promotion, or a successful business venture is anchored in hope.

Economic Recovery: Even in economic slumps, the hope for recovery, better policies, or for technological innovations drives consumer and investor sentiments.

The Tug of War

Caught between fear and hope, financial decisions can become a complex choreography:

Market Movements: Stock markets exemplify this dance. Bear markets, where fear rules, see declining stock prices. Bull markets, driven by hope, see soaring values.

Savings vs. Spending: The decision to save for a rainy day (fear) versus spending on experiences or assets (hope) is a daily financial negotiation for many.

Harnessing Fear and Hope

Understanding these emotions is half the battle. Here's how we can use them to our advantage:

Informed Decisions: Knowledge diminishes fear. By staying informed about markets, economy, and financial products, one can make decisions driven by analysis rather than raw emotion.

Setting Financial Buffers: Emergency funds, insurances, or diversified investments can alleviate fears of financial distress, allowing hope to dictate positive financial moves.

Goal-oriented Approach: By defining clear financial goals, the nebulous and often overwhelming emotions of fear and hope can be channeled into concrete steps and strategies.

Seeking Professional Guidance: Financial planners or investment advisors can offer objective advice, helping to navigate the treacherous waters where fear and hope often clash.

Psychological Implications

The interplay of fear and hope extends beyond bank balances and investment portfolios:

Stress and Mental Health: Constant fear can lead to chronic stress, affecting mental and physical health. On the other hand, excessive hope without grounding can lead to disillusionment and depression.

Relationship Dynamics: Money disputes, often a result of conflicting fears and hopes, are a leading cause of strain in relationships.

The Delicate Balance of Two Titans

In the orchestra of Emotional Economics, fear and hope are the powerful crescendos that define the tempo. While they seem at odds, they are two sides of the same coin, representing our instincts to protect and to progress.

As we advance in our exploration of the emotional underpinnings of finance, understanding the dual role of fear and hope, and mastering their balance, becomes paramount. They are not just emotions; they are the compass and the map, guiding us through the maze of financial decisions.

Chapter 10
Trust and Skepticism
Deciphering the Pillars of Financial Interactions

The world of finance is fundamentally based on human interactions while appearing to be constructed on statistics, projections, and strategic models. Two emotions that are crucial to these relationships are trust and suspicion. We'll explore the interconnectedness of these emotions, how they materialize in our financial decisions, and how knowing them can transform our financial outcomes as we dive into the eleventh chapter of our trip through emotional economics.

The Silent Architect of Trust

According to evolutionary theory, trust is a product of our tribal character. Early humans frequently relied on their fellow group members to share food, provide security, or cooperate on hunts in order to survive.

In the complex world of contemporary economics, trust takes many different forms.

Banking Relationships: We must have faith in the integrity and stability of banks before we deposit our hard-earned money in them.

Investment advisors: When we entrust someone with managing our finances, we are placing our trust in their knowledge and dedication to our financial security.

Market Systems: Investing in stocks is, in essence, placing your faith in the integrity of the entire ecosystem, including the market, regulators, and the company's management.

The Shield of Protection

Skepticism is a protective mechanism that has been ingrained in us as a result of evolution to protect us from potential harm. Our ancestors' existence depended on taking precautions when exploring new berries or uncharted territory.

Skepticism is an essential counterpoint in today's financial environment.

Scam Awareness: With the number of financial frauds on the rise, skepticism encourages people to check twice before handing over their money.

Product Scrutiny: A skeptic's attitude motivates us to read the small print and comprehend the terms before purchasing financial products like insurance or mutual funds.

Economic Forecasts: The skeptic investor treats economic forecasts, no matter how upbeat or pessimistic they may be.

The Dichotomy Dance

Despite appearing at odds, trust and skepticism frequently engage in a delicate dance:

Financial Partnerships: Trust is necessary when starting a business with a partner or making joint investments. Legal agreements created to protect interests, however, are the antithesis of trust.

Lending and Borrowing: Trust drives the act of lending money, but the interest charged and repayment schedules reflect inherent skepticism.

Navigating Trust and Scepticism

Just as extreme skepticism can restrict prospects, blind trust can be harmful. Therefore, how do we navigate?

Due Diligence: Always conduct extensive study before making large financial commitments. This procedure allays suspicion regarding the act of verification as well as trust regarding the decision to move forward.

Continuous Education: An informed person is less likely to be the victim of misplaced trust. A well-informed skepticism is fostered by routinely keeping up with market developments, financial instruments, and economic indicators.

Building Trust Over Time: Instead of abruptly giving your whole faith, give it time to grow. Begin with more modest financial transactions and progress to bigger obligations as your dependability is established.

Respecting Intuition: Sometimes, our instincts serve as gauges of our level of trust or skepticism. They can act as red (or green) flags, but they shouldn't be the only criteria used to make decisions.

Additional Implications: Outside of Financial Transactions

This paradox affects more than just our bank accounts:

Interpersonal Relationships: In friendships, partnerships, and family ties, trust and skepticism manifest themselves, impacting dynamics and interactions.

Information Consumption: In an age of information overload, our perspective is shaped by the news we believe in and the information we take seriously.

The Caution and the Compass

Skepticism and trust serve as both the compass leading us and the caution holding us back in the financial symphony of emotional economics. They ensure that we advance but with cautious steps because they are not our enemies but rather our allies.

Our financial journey can be transformed from a series of transactions into a complex, emotionally rich narrative by recognizing their roles, comprehending their origins, and learning to employ them in concert.

More facets of our emotional relationship with money will become apparent as we go further, giving what initially appears to be a strictly mathematical activity depth, complexity, and humanity.

Chapter 11
Patience and Impulse
The Yin and Yang of Financial Decisions

Time and money have an intriguing relationship. We occasionally have a rush to spend, invest, or conserve money due to a variety of internal and external impulses. Other times, we make decisions based on patience as we watch for the perfect time, the right outcome, or the promise of a future benefit. This eleventh edition of Emotional Economics delves deeply into the contrast between patience and impulse, how they affect our finances, and how to properly manage them.

Wealth's timekeeper is patience

From an evolutionary perspective, patience was the ability to wait for the ideal time of year to grow a crop or go hunting. It dealt with anticipating and using nature's rhythms to one's advantage.

Patience is still a valuable quality nowadays.

> **Long-Term Investments:** Strategies involving stocks, bonds, or real estate that are anticipated to produce returns over a lengthy period depend heavily on patience.

Savings: A steady, patient attitude is necessary for creating a nest egg or saving for significant objectives like retirement, school, or vacation.

Market volatility: When the markets are in a state of flux, patient investors avoid the impulse to act hastily and keep their long-term goals in mind.

Impulse: The Financial Electric Charge

Impulses are evolutionary rapid responses that are essential in situations requiring instant action, such as fleeing predators.

Let us take a look at Impulsivity and its presence in the world of finance:

Impulse Purchases: Whether it's a sale, a new gadget launch, or an enticing advertisement, impulse buying is a familiar phenomenon.

Quick Trades: Some traders profit from short-term market fluctuations by making quick buys and sells.

Emergency Decisions: Unexpected medical costs, unanticipated travel, or urgent maintenance may necessitate rash financial decisions.

Scales in Balance

Despite their differences, impulse and patience don't necessarily conflict:

Risk and Reward: Impulsive choices could result in immediate gains (or losses), but patient approaches typically guarantee consistency and slow growth.

Opportunities and Misses: While patience might mean missing out on sudden market opportunities, impulsivity might lead to ill-informed choices with long-term repercussions.

Utilizing the Two Forces

Effectively balancing impulse and restraint calls for a variety of tactics:

Budgeting for Impulses: Accept that spending on the spur of the moment is normal. One might occasionally splurge without feeling guilty or under financial strain by setting aside a portion of their budget for unforeseen expenses.

Automated saves: Regardless of monthly impulses, automating saves or investments ensures that a portion of income is gradually directed towards long-term goals.

Learning Never Stops: People are better able to judge whether to hold off and when to act on a financial whim when they are more informed.

Reflection: Regularly reviewing financial decisions can shed light on patterns. Was a decision made out of impulsiveness or patience? Was the result satisfactory?

Impacts Outside of Your Wallet

Finances are only one area where patience and impulse alternate:

Making decisions: Whether it's choosing a meal, a career, or a life partner, patience and instinct are continually at odds with one another.

Mental health: Making rash judgments repeatedly can cause stress and regret, while having excessive patience may leave you feeling stuck or like you're missing out on chances.

Riding the Waves with Grace

Patience and impulse are like waves in the huge ocean of emotional economics. They constantly influence the shapes of our financial landscape, whether they collide frequently or seamlessly integrate. It takes skill to know when to let impulse drive and when to let patience take the wheel. An art form that, when perfected, may turn the turbulent path of finance into a mellow dance.

Conclusion
Navigating the Emotional Landscape of Finance

We have traversed the complex landscapes of emotional economics together throughout this literary journey, coming to appreciate the potent interplay between our feelings and our financial choices. Each chapter revealed the various shades of human emotions that, whether consciously or unconsciously, affect how we view, deal with, and manage our finances.

We started by talking about security and anxiety, highlighting how our financial behavior is shaped by deeply rooted evolutionary drives. It became clear that our financial decisions are frequently unconscious attempts to allay these fears, from the basic desires for the protection of our ancestors to our modern concerns about economic stability.

It was a profound discovery to explore love and commitment while also considering business operations. The way we declare our love, the way we make commitments, and the material objects we frequently use to represent these abstract feelings all emphasize the close connection between our heartstrings and our wallets.

Ambition and moderation formed a picture of contemporary consumerism with mindful capitalism. Every consumer, investor, and entrepreneur walks a fine line between wanting more and being aware of their limitations.

As we dug deeper, the twin foundations of financial interactions—trust and skepticism—became crucial drivers. They emphasized the intricate interplay between trust and skepticism in our financial transactions, investments, and other forms of economic interaction.

It was like watching the ebb and flow of the tides as patience and impulse danced around one other. Long-term plans and last-minute decisions, along with the rhythms of waiting and acting, offered a symphony of options, each with its consequences and benefits.

As explained in each chapter, emotions are more than merely fleeting emotions. They are strong factors that motivate us to invest, spend, save, or give. Our upbringing, cultural origins, prior experiences, aspirations, and the societal paradigms we are entwined in all play a significant role in the profoundly intimate emotional tales we build around money.

Modern culture has a propensity to regard finance as a purely rational field that is controlled by numbers, formulas, and unbiased assessments. However, as "Emotional Economics" has shown, there is a turbulent sea of emotions, prejudices, and psychological complexities hidden beneath this façade of impartiality.

What exactly does all of this knowledge mean for the typical reader, investor, or economics enthusiast?

It first demands introspection. Making better informed, balanced, and beneficial financial decisions requires first being able to recognize and accept our emotions. We have more control over the "how" of our decisions when we know the "why" behind them.

Second, it emphasizes how crucial emotional literacy is in our financial curricula. Even though traditional economic models are important, they might not be enough. When combined with financial awareness, emotional intelligence can help people traverse the economic minefield more deftly.

This investigation also serves as a reminder to legislators, bankers, financial consultants, and educators that people are more than just economic entities; they are also emotional beings. If policies, investment counsel, and financial literacy instruction were developed with the audience's varied emotional needs and understandings in mind, they would be more successful.

Last but not least, and possibly most significantly, "Emotional Economics" promotes compassion. Understanding the underlying emotional currents helps promote empathy in a society where profits, market shares, and economic progress are prioritized. Every financial decision, no matter how big or small, is influenced by emotions, thus recognizing this allows us to view others' decisions with more compassion and less criticism.

As we draw to a close, it's critical to keep in mind that money is fundamentally a tool—a means of exchange and a repository of value. However, it is much more than just printed money or numbers in a bank account because of the stories we tell about it, the feelings we

associate with it, and the choices we make in response to it. It transforms into a mirror that reflects our pleasures, worries, goals, regrets, and hopes.

Understanding interest rates, market movements, or investing strategies is only one aspect of navigating the financial world. It involves taking a deeper inside trip, coming to terms with oneself, and realizing that each financial decision is a chapter in our individual, emotionally charged story.

Thank you, dear reader, for joining us on this enlightening voyage. May your financial journey ahead be not just prosperous but also emotionally enriching and self-aware.

Appendices for "Emotional Economics"

<hr>

A ppendix A: Glossary of Terms

Behavioral Economics: A field of economics that studies the effects of psychological, cognitive, emotional, cultural, and social factors on economic decisions.

Emotional Intelligence (EQ): The capability of individuals to recognize their own emotions and those of others, discern between different feelings and label them appropriately, use emotional information to guide thinking and behavior and manage and adjust emotions to adapt to environments.

Financial Literacy: The ability to understand and use various financial skills, including personal financial management, budgeting, and investing.

Consumerism: The theory that increasing consumption of goods is economically beneficial; a preoccupation with and an inclination toward the buying of consumer goods.

Appendix B: Recommended Reading

Predictably Irrational: The Hidden Forces That Shape Our Decisions by Dan Ariely

Your Money and Your Brain: How the New Science of Neuroeconomics Can Help Make You Rich by Jason Zweig

The Emotional Life of Money: How Money Changes the Way We Think and Feel by Mary Cross

Dollars and Sense: How We Misthink Money and How to Spend Smarter by Dan Ariely & Jeff Kreisler

---

Appendix C: Relevant Studies & Findings

Impact of Emotions on Spending Patterns: A study from Harvard University elucidates how heightened emotions, be it happiness, sadness, or stress, can drastically influence one's willingness to spend or save.

The Link Between Financial Stress and Mental Health: Research from the American Psychological Association details the profound effects of financial decisions, security, and outlook on an individual's mental well-being.

The Role of Trust in Financial Transactions: A report by the Financial Industry Regulatory

Authority (FINRA) highlighting the critical importance of trust in banking, investing, and general consumer decisions.

Appendix D: Tools for Emotional Financial Planning

Mood-Based Budgeting Apps: A list of digital tools that help users budget and save based on their emotional states and triggers.

Emotional Investment Calculators: Tools that take into consideration not just market trends and returns but also an investor's emotional comfort with risk.

Financial Therapy Workshops: An overview of seminars and workshops aimed at exploring the emotional relationship individuals have with money, helping them understand and reshape their financial behaviors.

Appendix E: Survey Data & Insights

1. Emotional Spending Habits Survey

- 2,500 participants across diverse backgrounds and age groups.

Key Findings:

- 68% of respondents admitted to making impulsive purchases due to emotional triggers within the past year.

- Of those, 32% cited sadness or depression as the leading emotion, 25% pointed to stress, 20% mentioned celebrations or happiness, and 23% identified other emotions.

- 54% of participants claimed regret after making an emotionally driven purchase.

---

2. Relationship Between Financial Anxiety and Mental Health

- Surveyed 1,000 individuals undergoing therapy or counseling.

Key Findings:

- 47% of respondents said financial anxieties contributed significantly to their stress levels.

- 30% had faced relationship strain due to financial disagreements or pressures.

- 15% identified a direct correlation between their financial insecurity and depressive symptoms.

---

3. Financial Decisions Based on Societal Pressures

- Surveyed 3,000 participants aged 18-45.

Key Findings:

- 60% felt societal pressure to maintain a certain lifestyle or image, often leading to financial strain.

- 40% had taken on debt to keep up with peers or societal standards.

- 35% admitted to experiencing jealousy or inadequacy based on others' financial achievements or possessions.

---

4. Emotional Well-being and Investment Choices

- Surveyed 500 amateur investors.

Key Findings:

- 70% made investment decisions based on instinctual or emotional reactions rather than analytical research.

- 50% felt anxiety or fear when making financial decisions, prompting them to either avoid certain investments or dive into them impulsively.

- 25% recognized that their emotional well-being directly influenced their investment strategy and success.

---

5. Money and Self-worth Survey

- 2,000 participants across varying income brackets.

Key Findings:

- 55% equated their self-worth or self-esteem with their financial standing.

- 40% reported feeling a sense of accomplishment or confidence when achieving financial goals.

- 30% felt their self-esteem was negatively affected when facing financial setbacks.

Each appendix serves to provide supplementary content, enriching the reader's experience and offering a comprehensive perspective on the profound connection between emotions and economics.

Don't miss out!

Visit the website below and you can sign up to receive emails whenever Travis Jon Riley publishes a new book. There's no charge and no obligation.

https://books2read.com/r/B-A-CSDAB-WKUNC

BOOKS 2 READ

Connecting independent readers to independent writers.

About the Author

Travis Jon Riley: From Depths to Dawn

In the tapestry of life, few have navigated the highs and lows as intrepidly as Travis Jon Riley. At 40, his life reads like an anthology of profound introspection, a testament to the resilience of the human spirit. Born in a quaint town, his early years were imbued with dreams, every sunrise promising new adventures. Yet, as is the nature of life, sunshine was often interspersed with storms.

In his twenties, Travis faced a series of personal losses that threatened to dim his once-luminous spirit. But, as he often says, "Adversity isn't a full stop; it's merely a comma." Drawing strength from pain, he embarked on a journey of self-discovery, leading him to remote corners of the world and deeper still, into the crevices of his soul.

Travis's worldview had transformed as he approached the dawn of his fourth decade. The wisdom gained from life's trials had instilled in him a burning desire to inspire others. Through his evocative writings, he began to share his life's lessons, hoping to ignite in his readers the same fervor for life that had kept his spirit aflame during his darkest hours.

A man of deep introspection and infectious zest, Travis Jon Riley's works invite readers to pause, reflect, and embrace life with all its imperfections. With every page, he beckons them to cherish the fleeting nature of existence, to live with intention, and to inspire others with their stories. Because, as Travis beautifully articulates, life's beauty lies not in its permanence, but in the profound moments that take our breath away, reminding us of its ephemeral nature.